Saint Jeanne Jugan

Saint Jeanne Jugan

God's Tenderness for the World

Éloi Leclerc

Translated by Patricia Kelly

DARTON · LONGMAN + TODD

English translation first published in 2009 by
Darton, Longman and Todd Ltd
1 Spencer Court
140–142 Wandsworth High Street
London
SW18 4JJ

First published in 2009 under the title *Sainte Jeanne Jugan: Tendresse de Dieu pour la Terre* by Desclée de Brouwer, 47, rue de Charenton, Paris

Illustrations taken from an icon by George Pinecross, photographed by Willy Berré.

ISBN 978–0–232–52778–0

A catalogue record for this book is available from the British Library.

Typeset by Kerrypress Ltd, Luton, Bedfordshire

Printed and bound by Progress Press, Malta

Contents

Preface

By canonising Jeanne Jugan, Sister Mary of the Cross in religion, the Church is proclaiming her holiness. But who was Jeanne? Very few people really know her, not because she lived her life far from us, in either time or space, but because she effaced herself behind her work.

The work of the Little Sisters of the Poor, who look after the poorest elderly folk in their Homes, is well known; but their Foundress remains in the shadows.

This little book about Jeanne seeks to draw her out of the shadows, first of all, by reviewing the unfolding of her life – the events which influenced her from her birth in 1792 into a simple fisherman's family in Cancale, until her death in 1879 at La Tour Saint-Joseph in Saint-Pern. We will see how the work to which Jeanne totally dedicated herself was born, then developed, and how she saw it snatched away. She was condemned to inactivity and forgotten about for the last twenty-three years of her life at La Tour Saint-Joseph.

But we cannot stop there. Jeanne's story leads us quite naturally to wonder, in the second part of the book, about the secret of her life. How can we not be amazed by this woman who, incredibly gifted for action, allowed herself, without rebelling, to be robbed of her work, and who, in silence and oblivion, managed to bloom in her interior life, like a rose in the desert? We will have to enter into Jeanne's secret to discover the meaning of her life and the source of her dynamism.

In canonising Jeanne, the Church seeks to set its seal on the authenticity of God's work in her. It recognises the work of the Holy Spirit in her life, and makes us see how Jeanne herself became this work; and it offers this eminently evangelical figure to our times, as a grace from the Lord, and as an example to be followed.

Part I

A life reviewed
1792–1879

Part I

A life reviewed
1792–1879

A sea-faring place

Cancale, a fishing port on the English Channel, west of the Bay of Mont-Saint-Michel, is where Jeanne Jugan, the girl who would be the Foundress of the Little Sisters of the Poor, was born in 1792, in the throes of the French Revolution.

At that time, Cancale had just over three thousand inhabitants, nine hundred of whom were gathered in the area called La Houle, bordering the harbour. More than seventy-five percent of the population lived off the sea. Some hundred small fishing boats bobbed up and down in the harbour; oysters and small fish were caught in the bay, while larger vessels went to fish for cod off the coast of Newfoundland, and yet others criss-crossed the seas of the globe to trade.

The people of Cancale, with their weather-beaten complexions, have always been exposed to the elements,

© Willy Berré

The young Jeanne takes the cattle to pasture, on the hills overlooking the bay of Mont-Saint-Michel.

Her birthplace and the chapel of Notre-Dame du Verger.

their candid gaze turned towards the broad horizon; a small community, entrepreneurial, tenacious, and proud.

A humble cottage

In those troubled days of the French Revolution known as the Terror, tenacity and pride had a special name in those Breton lands – fidelity.

This was a fidelity lived out in the shadows, rooted in hearts, as it was in a humble cottage in the midst of fields in the hamlet of Petites Croix, not far from the town of Cancale. There, into this poor household, a baby girl, the sixth child of Marie Horel, wife of Joseph Joucan (Jugan), came into the world on 25 October 1792. Baptized the very same day, the child was given the name Jeanne. There was great joy that day in the hamlet of Petites Croix; but great anxiety, too, for the father was absent. He had left for Newfoundland on 25 April, and would only come back on 12 November.

A poor family

Jeanne grew up, laughing and playing with children of her own age. But she became acquainted with sadness and suffering early on. Four of her brothers and sisters died in infancy; and in 1796 her father, once more away at sea, did not come back, and nor would he ever return. The family was poor, sometimes lacking even the basics. Her mother worked long days, and the young Jeanne led the cattle to pasture on the hills which overlooked the bay of Mont-Saint-Michel.

The dawning of Jeanne's faith

Gradually the terrors of the Revolution faded away. In 1802, the parish church was re-opened for worship. Jeanne was ten years old. The date of her First Holy Communion is unknown. What religious formation did she receive? Her mother taught her to pray and to recite the rosary; and perhaps she also benefited from the secret catechism classes offered by the Tertiaries of Saint John Eudes.

Around the age of fifteen or sixteen, Jeanne was placed as a kitchen-maid in La Mettrie-aux-Chouettes, near Cancale. Madame de La Choüe welcomed her warmly into her home, a traditional Saint-Malo ship-owner's country house. Employed in the kitchen, she was also involved in helping the poor, and visiting local families and lonely old folk.

In 1816 a major parish mission was preached in Cancale over three weeks. Jeanne followed it reverently and fervently.

'God wants me for himself'

Jeanne was now twenty-four years old. She was a pretty young woman, tall and slender. Her face had even features, and she had shining eyes and a beautiful smile. A young sailor wanted to marry her, but Jeanne turned him down.

Deep within her she heard a call. She talked seriously about it to her mother, 'God wants me for himself. He is keeping me for a work which is not yet known, not yet founded.'

This inspiration, this call, so like the call of the open sea – where did it come from? The women of Cancale were strong; they were also big-hearted. As soon as one of them needed help, the neighbours hurried to offer it. Jeanne had experienced this for herself many times. She, too, had a big heart – a heart as wide as the sea. This was the heart which God wanted for himself, which he was keeping for a love as wide as the world.

Saint-Servan: working at the hospital of Le Rosais

Sometime in 1817, Jeanne left the family home and went to live alone in Saint-Servan, a village near Saint-Malo. She left anything that was elegant behind with her sisters. She still did not know what God wanted from her, but she was drawn to serving the poor.

At that time, there was no lack of poor people in the village of Saint-Servan, with more than half the population living below the poverty line. Jeanne entered the hospital of Le Rosais as a nurse. This was the only hospital in the town, overflowing with the sick and the destitute; Jeanne looked after them for six years.

A parish mission, preached at the church in Saint-Servan over five weeks, helped Jeanne to deepen her faith. At that time she belonged to the Third Order founded by Saint John Eudes, whose spirituality was totally directed towards a loving relationship with the Lord and a 'tender and active' charity to all.

Waiting

Serious fatigue forced Jeanne to quit her work at the hospital of Le Rosais. Mademoiselle Lecoq, a lady from

This is the heart which God wants for himself,
which he was keeping for a love as wide as the world.

Jeanne working in the hospital of Le Rosais.

Saint-Servan who was twenty years her senior, took her into her home as a companion and maid. The years passed; and still Jeanne did not know what this unknown work was, for which God had destined her.

On the death of her employer in 1835, she and a friend, Françoise Aubert, rented accommodation in the centre of Saint-Servan. Soon a young woman of seventeen, Virginie Trédaniel, came to live with them. The three of them lived a life of prayer and charity, Jeanne doing the house-work and the washing.

The winter of 1839–1840 – God's hour

At the start of the winter of 1839, Jeanne was forty-seven years old. The cold northern winds were blowing in from the sea when Jeanne discovered an aged woman in dire straits, blind, infirm and abandoned. Her heart was moved. Now was the moment when God gave her a sign. With the agreement of her two companions, she decided to take the old woman into her home, giving up her own bed, while she went up to the attic to sleep.

A gap had just opened in her life into which the Breath of God would sweep, with all the distress and loneliness of suffering humanity. A great adventure began, humbly, without discussion, without fuss, in a deprived garret. Soon a second poor woman was welcomed, then a third.

A friend of Virginie Trédaniel's, Marie Jamet, came to support them with her help. She wasted no time in joining the group. Another young woman, Madeleine Bourges, initially taken in when sick, became a precious help once she had recovered. Charity was truly contagious! In this way a charitable association was formed, which adopted a rule of life inspired by the Third Order founded by Saint John Eudes.

The small community, with its rule of life, found support in the person of the young parish priest of Saint-Servan, Fr Le Pailleur, who became their chaplain. He would be an effective support, but also, for Jeanne, a source of great ordeals.

Recourse to begging

In 1841, as the number of elderly people they rescued continued to grow, the three friends rented a house, Le Grand-en-Bas; but shortly even this was not large enough.

So, with the help of Fr Le Pailleur, Jeanne acquired the former convent of the Daughters of the Cross, not far from the parish church. Encouraged by the Brothers of St John of God, she began her begging rounds. 'It cost me', she said later, 'but I did it for God, and for the poor.' It was said that one day, an old bachelor, who was annoyed, slapped her. She replied, gently, 'Thank you; that slap was for me. Now, please give me something for my poor!'

The birth of a community

On 29 May 1842, gathered around Fr Le Pailleur, the small association clarified its rule of life, which was inspired by the rule of the Brothers of St John of God. They chose Jeanne as their superior. This was the first stage in the formation of a new community.

The following year, in 1843, Jeanne was re-elected as superior. But in a dramatic turn of events, Fr Le Pailleur quashed the election on his own authority and replaced Jeanne with Marie Jamet – shy, younger, and more malleable. Jeanne bowed to his wishes. Unperturbed, she carried on, borne forward by her great heart. The work was begun, and nothing could stop it. In fact, it was no

longer Jeanne who loved and who acted, but the love of
God himself which, through her, was spread throughout
the world.

From the attic to the Académie française: the Prix Montyon

The work would undergo a swift and surprising growth.
It responded to a great need at that time: that society had
nothing for elderly people with no resources of their
own. There were no pensions, no Social Security, no care
homes. There was no provision at all. Jeanne's initiative
came from a prophetic intuition. She was farsighted. For
her it was not just a question of giving poor elderly folk a
home, and feeding them, but rather of giving them
respect, consideration, and love.

As soon as it became known, the work was applauded
in the highest places. On 11 December 1845, the
Académie française granted Jeanne the Prix Montyon.
Under the dome of the Academy building, before a
renowned audience, which included among others the
writers Chateaubriand and Victor Hugo, the poet and
politician Lamartine, and the historians and politicians
Thiers and Guizot, Monsieur André Dupin gave a

© Willy Berré

It was no longer Jeanne who loved and who acted, but the love of God himself which, through her, was spread throughout the world.

The first community of four, with Jeanne as superior.

powerful eulogy about Jeanne. He ended his speech by saying, 'How has Jeanne been able to meet all the expenses? What can I say, gentlemen? Providence is great. Jeanne has her prayers; Jeanne has her tears; Jeanne has her work; Jeanne always carries on her arm the basket which she invariably brings home full. What a saintly woman! Into your basket, the Académie puts what it can: it grants you the sum of three thousand francs!'

The press soon echoed this homage; even the Masonic Lodge joined in the praise. In 1848, Louis Veuillot published a long article in *L'Univers* on Jeanne's work.

'I believed I was in the presence of a superior being'

In 1846, an English visitor, drawn by Jeanne's reputation, went to visit her at Dinan. Impressed, he wrote, 'There is something so calm and saintly in this woman that, when I saw her, I believed I was in the presence of a superior being. [...] I told her that, after having journeyed through France, she should come to England to teach us how to care for the poor; she replied that, God willing, she would go if she were invited.'

A torrent of foundations

From 1846 to 1852 there was a veritable torrent of foundations. Houses were opened in Rennes, Dinan, Tours, Paris, Nantes, Besançon, Angers, Bordeaux, Rouen, and Nancy.

In the meantime, Jeanne, advised by Fr Félix Massot, the former Provincial of the Hospitaller Order of the Brothers of St John of God, drew up a more detailed rule. In 1849 the Congregation definitively adopted the popular name *Little Sisters of the Poor*.

In 1851, the first house was opened in England.

Jeanne present everywhere

During these years, Jeanne was present everywhere. Tireless, she hastened from one city to another. Here she opened a home; there she brought help to a foundation in difficulty. She answered the slightest appeal. She was the person whom public opinion knew and celebrated.

By 1850 there were more than a hundred Little Sisters, in eleven homes, looking after eleven hundred elderly people.

There is something so calm and saintly in this woman.

*Jeanne received the Prix Montyon for her work
on behalf of poor elderly people.*

Halted

Jeanne's work, and her growing popularity, worried Fr Le Pailleur; they offended him. He so wanted to be considered the founder of the work. However, this seemed to elude him.

In 1853 Jeanne was called to Rennes where the Mother-house and novitiate were then situated. Fr Le Pailleur asked her to stop all external work, and to cease all contact with benefactors. In future she was to regard herself as a simple Sister, with no authority or responsibility. From now on she would only be known by her name in religion, Sister Mary of the Cross.

Jeanne obeyed without protest. Henceforth everything in the Congregation would be decided without her. Four years were spent in the silence of La Piletière, in Rennes. The work nevertheless continued to grow, in France and abroad, with the providential help of Fr Ernest Lelièvre, a priest from the Nord region of France, who dedicated himself totally to the work of the Little Sisters. In 1854 the Congregation numbered five hundred Little Sisters and thirty-six homes.

1856: La Tour in Saint-Pern

The number of novices continued to grow. The Little Sisters acquired the property of La Tour in Saint-Pern, thirty-five kilometres north-west of Rennes, for the Mother-house and novitiate.

Jeanne, too, had to go to La Tour. She did not stay in the part reserved for the superiors; banished to live among the novices, she shared in their life.

The Desert ...

Deprived of any external work, stripped of all responsibility, removed from the General Council, and condemned to silence and oblivion, Jeanne found herself quite insignificant in this huge property, far from the city where she had friends and acquaintances. Everything was taken from her. It was the desert.

She was still too large-hearted for any self-absorption. She also had the companionship of the novices, whom she loved. There was no complaint, and no bitterness, in this heart which knew only generosity.

However, Jeanne was quite clear-sighted. One day, she said to Fr Le Pailleur, 'You have stolen my work from me.

But I give it to you willingly.' Such detachment was not without suffering. She said to a friend who had come to visit her, 'Do not call me Jeanne any more, but Sister Mary of the Cross.' Her friend gazed at her. Jeanne was silent: Mary's silence at the foot of the cross.

She was not dealt with considerately at La Tour. When the novices were taught the history of the Congregation, her name was not mentioned. She did not exist. The founder was Fr Le Pailleur, and everyone had to be made aware of this. One day, a novice learned from her parents about the true origins of the Congregation and Jeanne's important role, and came to ask her about it. Jeanne simply replied, 'Make the most of your novitiate, be fervent and faithful to our holy rule.' And then she added, 'You will never know what it cost.'

No one would ever know 'what it cost'; this would remain Jeanne's secret. She could have objected and appealed to a higher authority. But Jeanne preferred to remain silent. She allowed herself to be stripped of what was dearest to her – her work, the work for which God had destined her. She understood, in silence and in patience, that now God was asking her to give herself totally to him, so that she herself would become God's work, in great poverty of spirit.

… and the Rose

People who have achieved great things and who have known success and renown often suffer a kind of interior collapse when, for whatever reason, they have all work and all responsibility taken away from them. Banished to the shadows of oblivion, they feel as though they have been thrown into a great abyss. Now they are just flotsam, sometimes, bitter flotsam.

This was not what happened with Jeanne, for her life was based on interior riches. The calm and serenity which she demonstrated throughout these twenty-seven years in the desert revealed the solidity of her faith, and the depth of her heart, made for loving, incapable of turning in on itself.

St Luke the Evangelist wrote about Jesus that, 'His reputation continued to grow, and large crowds would gather to hear him and to have their sickness cured, but he would always go off to some place where he could be alone and pray' (Luke 5.15–16). Jeanne followed this

She lived completely in the present,
attentive to those around her.

Jeanne healing a sick child

example. She was often to be seen withdrawing on her own to the fields or the woods, her rosary in her hand. Her desert flowered.

Jeanne never retreated into nostalgia. She had placed the future in God's hands. She lived completely in the present, attentive to those who were around her, and to all the great intentions of the Church in her day. The novices amongst whom she lived were the primary beneficiaries of her concern. She was totally devoted to them, always ready to help them in their search for the Lord.

She was also able to admire the beauty of the simplest things. She was quick to stop in front of a rose in the garden. Its silent beauty filled her with a secret joy. It never spoke its name, and was not eager to be known or acknowledged. Just a pure reflection of the beauty which is above all names, it quite simply flowered.

One day Jeanne was showing a novice the wild rose bushes which were in the courtyard of the novitiate, and said to her, 'You see these roses? They are growing wild. You too are like a little wild flower, but if you let yourself be well formed, you will become a beautiful rose, transformed by God's love. But you have to allow yourself to be humiliated. Rather than turning in on yourself, rise up towards God.' What a marvellous definition of humility! Not turning in on oneself, retreating into oneself, but rising, opening up, blossoming like a rose. With this comment, Jeanne showed the secret of her life, the secret of the path which she followed.

One Christmas – becoming a child with the Christ-Child

On the afternoon of Christmas Day 1864, Jeanne was walking in the grounds of La Tour, meditating on the great mystery of this feast-day. On the way she met a group of young postulants, who quickly surrounded her. At this Jeanne allowed her interior joy to overflow. In the midst of these young women, who loved her, she started to sing with them a Christmas carol from her youth.

> *He is born, the divine Child,*
> *Play, you oboes, resound, you pipes,*
> *He is born, the divine Child,*
> *Let us sing about his birth.*

Jeanne radiated God's gentleness, and laughed with the clear laugh of a child. On this Christmas Day, Jeanne had become a child with the Christ-Child. She sang out her joy with these young women whom she had just met; and then she went on her way, continuing to sing, waving her stick joyfully, as though she were beating time, and inviting all creation to sing with her.

The ideals of the Little Sisters at stake

From the very beginning, the ideal of the Little Sisters of the Poor had been to live in poverty with the poor, only dependent upon the generosity of their benefactors, that is to say through the Collecting. This was a path of total confidence in God, lived out day by day. Jeanne had given them the example.

The English tourist who had visited her shortly after she had founded the home in Dinan had noted that, 'She did not know where the next day's provisions would come from, but she persevered in the firm conviction that God would never abandon the poor.'

Over time, the Congregation would be left more and more legacies, and the temptation to convert these legacies into a source of regular income was great. From a human point of view, this would give a certain security for the homes and for those living in them.

*She did not know where the next day's provisions
would come from, but she persevered in the firm conviction
that God would never abandon the poor.*

A scene from the Collecting.

A choice to be made

Should they commit to this path? In 1865, the question arose about a major legacy. The Comte de Bertou, a friend who had helped the Little Sisters with the financial management of their homes, laid their responsibilities clearly before them. They had to choose between the human path of security in having fixed income, and the path of begging, that is, of total trust in God, lived from day to day. In this case, legacies would have to be considered simply as gifts for their daily needs.

The moment of truth

The Little Sisters hesitated between the two paths. Aware of the gravity of what was at stake, and in desperation, they turned to Jeanne. They remembered the Little Sister in the shadows, the first Little Sister. This recourse to Jeanne in these circumstances was an implicit acknowledgement of her charism as Foundress.

Far from being triumphant, Jeanne was surprised and perplexed to see herself called to the 'Council': 'I am only a poor, uneducated person,' she said. 'What can I say?' Now that she had placed everything in God's hands, she felt that she had nothing more to add. Faced with the Sisters' insistence, she obeyed, and came to the 'Council'.

She gave her opinion: for her there was no hesitation. The way was clearly marked, the path of faith in God. Fixed income was to be relinquished.

Jeanne's opinion prevailed. The Congregation committed itself to not owning anything which could bring in an income. At the end of the official acts, signed by the Council members, Jeanne added her signature – the only signature, indeed, the only writing of hers which we have.

Once the meeting had ended, Jeanne returned to her path in the shadows. She went back to her place among the novices, immersing herself in the silence and oblivion, like a fish in water.

True foundations

When he deprived Jeanne of any external work and banished her to be with the novices, Fr Le Pailleur never suspected that he was giving her fertile ground where she could exercise her founding charism in silence, without anyone knowing about it, but in the most profound manner.

Real foundations are always hidden – they are deep in the earth. Through the influence of her life and her spirit, Jeanne marked with her charism all the young postulants and novices who passed through La Tour over those twenty-three years.

The peace of the evening

Many saints die young. They are not worn down by the ravages of time, and do not know the challenge of old age, with its infirmities, dependence, and loneliness.

In 1873, Jeanne, now aged eighty-one, was confined to bed for a few weeks. She recovered, but did not regain her strength. Moving around was now more and more painful, and she spent the last years of her life in a room in the infirmary.

Almost blind, she could no longer read or sew. She prayed, with her rosary in her hand. Her mind was still clear, her face more and more translucent, radiating serenity. 'When you are old,' she said to a novice one day,

'you won't see anything any more. I no longer see anything except the good God ... He sees me, and that's
enough.'

The sculptor Aimé-Jules Dalou (1838–1902) wanted
to express through his art this period of Jeanne's life, her
silent serenity and maturity at the end of her long jour-
ney towards God. He sculpted her sitting down,
wrapped in her big cape with its hood up, so that only her
face and hands are visible. Her face has fine, relaxed
features, and her eyes are lowered. Her right hand,
resting on her knee, is half open, to let the 'Invisible' in.
This is no longer Jeanne, the untiring seeker of bread for
the poor, with her basket on her arm, but Jeanne, God's
beggar, enveloped in the great cloak of his mercy. It is
evening; the evening of a life completely abandoned,
peacefully awaiting the moment of the blessed encoun-
ter.

At the door of the General Chapter

In July 1878, a year before Jeanne's death, the Little
Sisters held their General Chapter at La Tour. The thirty-
seven Capitulars met together, representing the one
hundred and seventy homes which then made up the

Congregation. A Chapter is always an important moment in the life of a religious institution, and the most solemn event is that of the election of a Superior General, whose task it will be to carry out the decisions of the Chapter.

This moment had come. In front of the door to the large room in which the election was taking place was a group of novices who were waiting for the door to be opened, ready to go in to intone the *Te Deum* in thanksgiving.

But the waiting dragged on ... Then – surprise! Supported by a Sister came Jeanne herself, smiling, amused to find herself too, at the door of the Chapter. The situation was quite surreal: the Foundress, the first Little Sister, aged eighty-six, waiting, like the youngest novice, for the door to the Chapter to be opened.

'Ah, yes,' said Jeanne to one of the astonished novices, 'I am here to wait with you ... However, I should be inside!'

In her heart, Jeanne was really waiting for another door to open before her, to sing another *Te Deum*, this time, the eternal one.

Real foundations are always hidden –
they are deep in the earth.

Pope Leo XIII approves the Constitutions.

But before this final threshold was crossed, Jeanne was given a great joy: on 1 March 1879, Pope Leo XIII approved the Constitutions of the Little Sisters for seven years.

1879: Jeanne's death. 'Eternal Father, open your doors today'

That same year summer came. Jeanne was steadily growing weaker. On 27 August, she made her last Confession. The next morning, after Mass, she collapsed. She recovered consciousness and received the Sacrament of the Sick. She was heard to murmur this prayer:

'Eternal Father, open your doors today to the most wretched of your little daughters, who so wants to see you.' And then she added, 'O Mary, my mother, come to me, you know that I love you and that I long to see you.'

These were her last words. She died quite peacefully at the age of eighty-seven. The door of the Kingdom of light and peace, promised to the little ones, had just opened up before her.

© Willy Berré

An angel bears Jeanne's soul to heaven.

Part II

The secret of
Jeanne's life

Part II

The secret of Jeanne's life

A woman of deeds

What strikes us at first about Jeanne's life, is, of course, her deeds and her work. With no resources and no publicity, this woman, who came from a very humble background, managed in a short space of time, to establish a whole network of homes in France and abroad for the elderly poor, and she was able to communicate her dynamism and her zeal to many people who were totally devoted to the same cause. This is amazing.

Resourceful, enterprising and a leader, Jeanne was a woman of action in every sense of the word. She did not give great speeches, or write any books. She acted.

This action was really creative and prophetic. Opening homes for the poorest elderly folk, where they were not only given a bed, fed, and looked after, but also given companionship and respect, was truly innovative in its day. At that time there were neither homes for the elderly nor Social Security. Poor people were left to themselves. By responding to a genuine social need,

Jeanne showed clear-sightedness and courage. She was very foresighted. During the ceremony for her beatification, Pope John Paul II emphasised this in his homily: 'You could say that she received from the Holy Spirit what may be called a prophetic intuition of the needs and deep desires of the elderly,' he said, clarifying that those needs and aspirations, received by Jeanne as a prophetic intuition, were 'their desire to be respected, esteemed, and loved; their fear of loneliness and at the same time their wish for a certain independence and privacy; their longing to feel themselves still useful; and, very often, a strong desire to deepen their life of faith and to live it more intensely.'

An active contemplative

From where did Jeanne draw her clear-sightedness and her courage?

When we wonder about the motivation for her action and the source of her creative intuitions, we very soon notice that her deeds were prompted by the inspiration of faith and love. It welled up from that interior place where Jeanne lived in deep communion with the God who once revealed himself as a 'Burning Bush'.

Her deeds were prompted
by the inspiration of faith and love.

Jeanne looks after the poor sick woman whom she has just
welcomed.

This communion with God, which is lived out as a gift of life offered freely and which, through her, sought to transmit itself, shine forth and act, was at the source of Jeanne's deeds and her intuition.

Jeanne worked with the innermost conviction that she was doing God's work. She was deeply supported by the strength of this love which compelled her to act.

God's work

Very early on, Jeanne had this innermost conviction that God was calling her to carry out a particular work. She was then only twenty-four years old. She had already explained to her mother, who was astonished that she had turned down an offer of marriage from a young sailor, that 'God wants me for himself. He is keeping me for a work which is not yet known.'

So what was this work? Jeanne did not yet know. She would wait for a long time, until the age of forty-seven, until God gave her a sign. She did not grow impatient. It was not up to her to invent a work. She simply had to remain available and ready to respond. And God silently prepared her. He had given her a big heart. This was one of her natural gifts, and it was soon remarked upon. At La

Mettrie-aux-Chouettes, where she was placed at the age
of fifteen or sixteen as a kitchen-maid, she was happy
when the lady of the house asked her to visit local
families or lonely old people in the neighbourhood. She
was glad to bring them some compassion and happiness
by her presence and her attention. When she went to
Saint-Servan, she committed herself to working with the
poorest sick people at the hospital of Le Rosais. Clearly,
there was something powerful within her which drove
her to care for those in distress.

Shortly after her arrival in Saint-Servan, Jeanne was
happy to follow a mission which was preached in the
parish church of Sainte-Croix. For her, this was a revelation of God's great love through the heart of Christ.
Jeanne's heart throbbed and glowed. A few years later
the moment would come when God, finally, gave her his
sign. This was at the start of the winter of 1839.

Jeanne discovered a poor woman who was blind and
infirm; she had just lost her sister, who was her only
support. She was now alone and abandoned. Jeanne was
moved, and took her into her own home. This act opened
up Jeanne's life to the great inspiration of God's love,
which would take her much further. Now she knew

what God wanted of her. There was no hesitation, no turning back. She went straight ahead, totally given to the work which God awaited from her. She took in a second person, and then a third. And God worked with her, giving her the necessary help; this was where Jeanne's boldness and clarity of vision came from.

A soul acting and 'acted upon'

It would clearly be wrong to present Jeanne as a woman who realised a purely humanitarian ideal thanks to her own strengths. On the contrary, in her the Christian mystic described by Henri Bergson in *The Two Sources of Morality and Religion* is brought to perfection. 'He has felt truth flowing into his soul from its fountain-head like an active force. He can no more help spreading it abroad than the sun can help diffusing its light. (p.199) [...] Let us say that henceforth for the soul there is a superabundance of life. There is a boundless impetus. There is an irresistible impulse which hurls it into vast enterprises. A calm exaltation of all its faculties makes it see things on a vast scale only, and, in spite of its own weakness, produce only what can be mightily wrought. Above all, it sees things simply, and this simplicity, which is equally striking in the words it uses and the conduct it follows, guides it through complications which it apparently does not even perceive. An innate knowledge, or rather an acquired ignorance, suggest to it straightaway the step to be taken, the decisive act, the unanswerable word. Yet effort remains indispensable, endurance and perseverance likewise. But they come of themselves, they develop of their own accord, in a soul acting and acted upon, whose liberty coincides with the divine activity. They represent a vast expenditure of energy, but this energy is supplied as it is required, for the superabundance of vitality which it demands flows from a spring which is the very source of life …' (p. 198)

A flood of life racing towards its Source

This life-force continued to inhabit and support Jeanne, even when she was being stripped of her work and forbidden any action, with all responsibilities within the Congregation which she had founded taken away from her. She suffered from seeing her work confiscated, but she did not break down, nor did she turn in on herself in bitterness. Neither did she rebel. The surge of life which had carried her forward now turned back, with the same strength, to its source, and Jeanne allowed herself to be

*A calm exaltation of all her faculties
meant that she discerned the whole and,
weak as she was, acted powerfully.*

carried. God was, therefore, still at work. But now it was Jeanne who became God's work.

A mystery of love and of poverty

Jeanne entered into this mystery of love and poverty, a mystery which she lived in silence, humility and adoration. It is hard to imagine a greater deprivation than that which Jeanne suffered. The Foundress of a work which drew the admiration of all, from journalists to the Académie française, and even the Masonic Lodge, Jeanne, her work brutally stripped from her, was banished to the lowest place, condemned to silence and oblivion.

She accepted this deprivation, which lasted twenty-seven years, until her death, without protest, but not without suffering.

It is never easy to accept being treated as though one is insignificant, particularly when one has accomplished such a great work! It is even more difficult to acknowledge God's hand in such injustice and, above all, to willingly accept as Jeanne did, never to see the face of a poor person again.

God was there, still at work.
But now it was Jeanne who had become God's work.

Jeanne pronounces her perpetual vows.

poverty, leading us towards that radical dispossession which surrenders a soul to God.

The grace of hospitality towards the Aged Poor, Jeanne Jugan's charism as Foundress, was welcomed by her with simplicity of soul. Pursuing her particular charism, she found in this vow a privileged means of expressing the gift of ourselves to our apostolate of charity. Consecrated hospitality is, in the midst of the world, a witness to the mercy of the Father and the compassionate love of the Heart of Jesus.

(Excerpts from the Constitutions of the Little Sisters of the Poor)

The Congregation of the Little Sisters of the Poor

Charism

The spirit of the Congregation is the evangelical spirit expressed by Jesus in the Beatitudes. Jeanne Jugan, faithful to the inspiration of the Holy Spirit, radiated particularly in her life gentleness and humility of heart, which enabled her to surrender herself, in simplicity, to the joy of hospitality. That is what our name Little Sisters of the Poor denotes.

For Jeanne Jugan, the Poor defined her vocation. God had waited for her in the Poor; she had met and found him in the Poor.

To be a Little Sister of the Poor, reminds the Little Sisters of those to whom they have vowed their lives, and of their desire to go always to the poorest, to create a flow of apostolic collaboration and fraternal charity, in order to assist Christ in the Poor. For each one personally, it is an invitation to share in the beatitude of spiritual

Bibliography

Sister Elisabeth Allard, *The Sayings of Jeanne Jugan*. London, Catholic Truth Society, 1980.

Henri Bergson, *The Two Sources of Morality and Religion*. Trans. R. Ashley Audra and Cloudesley Brereton with W. Horsfall Carter. London, Macmillan and Co., 1935.

Gabriel-Marie, Cardinal Garrone, *Poor in Spirit. The Spirituality of Jeanne Jugan*. Trans. Alan Neame. London, Darton, Longman & Todd, 2005.

Éloi Leclerc, *The Desert and the Rose. The Spirituality of Jeanne Jugan*. Trans. Clare Trocmé. London, Darton, Longman & Todd, 2002.

Paul Milcent, *Jeanne Jugan. Humble So As To Love More*. Trans. Alan Neame. London, Darton, Longman & Todd, 2000.

Marie-Hélène Sigaut and René Berthier, *At the Service of the Elderly. Jeanne Jugan and the Little Sisters of the Poor*. Trans. Charles Mann & the Little Sisters of the Poor. Toulouse, Les Éditeurs du Rameau, 1996.

Prayer through the intercession of Saint Jeanne Jugan

Jesus, you rejoiced and praised your Father for having revealed to little ones the mysteries of the Kingdom of Heaven. We thank you for the graces granted to your humble servant, Saint Jeanne Jugan, to whom we confide our petitions and needs.

Father of the Poor, you have never refused the prayer of the lowly. We ask you, therefore, to hear the petitions that she presents to you on our behalf.

Jesus, through Mary, your Mother and ours, we ask this of you, who live and reign with the Father and the Holy Spirit now and forever. Amen.

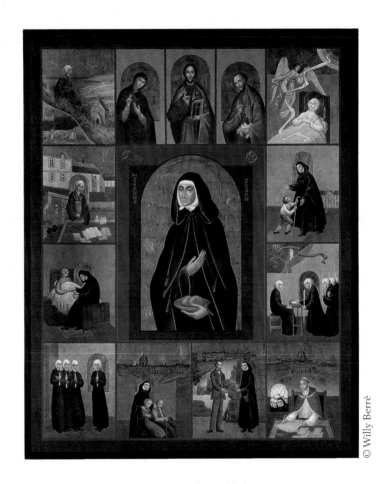

Blessed be God in all things!

Icon painted in 2004 by George Pinecross.

God,' she said repeatedly in the evening of her life, whilst the light of the Kingdom was already penetrating the innermost depths of her heart.

If Jeanne is canonised today and offered as an example, it is certainly not because she suffered humiliation and injustice – many others have known this awful fate – but because of the way in which she lived this humiliation and deprivation, which enabled the luminous work of God to be seen in her, in all its purity and radiance.

well organised it may be, is a sad place, sometimes
deathly sad. A poor person is not just a medical file to be
referred to from a distance.

'Making the poor happy' such is the charism of the
Little Sisters of the Poor. With no distinction between
them and the poor amongst whom they live, the Sisters
are called to be the revelation of God's compassion to
each one. They will be, in all humility, the marvellous
epiphany of God's Tenderness for the World, or they will
no longer truly be Little Sisters of the Poor.

The song of the poor: 'Blessed be God in all things!'

Jeanne had passed on her essential message, and now her
heart was wholly given to praise. It is not enough to say
that there was no bitterness or rancour in her heart. She
marvelled at all that was beautiful around her, at La Tour
and in the Congregation, doing so with even more joy
than if it were her own work. She admired the new
buildings, the totally new church, the growing number of
novices and the Congregation's expansion throughout
the world. Jeanne saw God's work in all of this, and her
heart rejoiced. It was the joy of the heart of the poor: a
joy expressed in praise. 'One must always say, Blessed be

But Jeanne understood that God was now asking her to give up the work to which she had totally dedicated herself: from now on, it was she herself who was called to become God's work.

The final, sublime message

Among the novices, sharing their day-to-day life, Jeanne, far from closing in on herself, influenced each of them, through the attention she gave them and her presence among them, by her spirit and her simplicity. She herself revealed to them and passed on to them her founding charism: 'Be little, make yourselves little,' she liked to say to them. In this way she explained quite simply to them what she lived herself and what made her so present and so close: being little, to be close to the least. 'Our happiness,' she would say, 'is to be a little sister to the poor. Making the poor happy is everything.'

The poor are not happy just because they are given a home, food and care, but also, above all, because, through the care they are given, they see that they are loved and worthy of consideration. Without this close relationship of love, which alone can lift someone out of loneliness and give them a name and a face, the home, however